LEICESTER'S TRAMS

by
Geoff Creese

C000261622

Cover. This ornate ironwork supporting the overhead electric wires stood in East Park Road at the junction of St. Peter's Road and Chesterfield Road, which led to the City General Hospital. Trams were still much in evidence and heavily used during their last winter of 1948/49; No.2 is on the clockwise East Park Road, circular route (No.2) climbing towards the Evington Road Shopping district, where the line narrowed to single track with several passing loops. Tram No.2 would eventually turn onto London Road at the Victoria Park Gates Junction and head downhill towards the LMS station and the city centre. Photo F.N.T. L.L. Jones.

Rear Cover. Reproduced from the 1936 edition of the Leicester City Transport official handbook, this map depicts the compact nature of the city at that time. With the exception of the Melbourne Road route – converted to bus operation on 13 December 1933 – the Tramway routes are shown at their zenith. Bus services are as yet a secondary operation, serving new housing estates built in the post-World War I years.

Above. Tram No.33 leaves Loughborough Road on the Belgrave Route in May 1949 bound for the Clock Tower. This junction with Melton Road was known as the Melton Turn. BBC 821 – a Hillman Minx – is well parked and it is hoped that the cable brakes worked on FOM 129. a Morgan 3 wheeler... Photograph National Tramway Museum.

Copyright Irwell Press
ISBN 1-903266-17-3
First published in the United Kingdom in 2000
by Irwell Press
59A, High Street, Clophill,
Bedfordshire MK45 4BE

Contents

Gallowtree Gate in 1938. Tram No.6, one of twenty-three rebuilt with extended lower deck frames, is on a Route 1 service to East Park Road via London Road, followed by car No.55 on Route 3 to Stoneygate. Both are still in the more ornate pre-1937 livery, with gold lining and numerals. The original legend 'Leicester Corporation Tramways' was altered to 'Leicester City Tramways' after 1919 and finally to Leicester City Transport in 1935 reflecting the increasing use of buses on new routes. Car parking was haphazard; JU7580, a 1935 Vauxhall 14 is parked outside J. Sainsburys, then simply 'a grocer'. Woolworths is the adjacent store where goods were priced at 3d or 6d. An LMS horsedrawn parcels van is 'parked' outside the Pelican pub; maybe the drayman is delivering supplies of tobacco and cigarettes to Newmans Ltd on the corner, leading to Horsefair Street.

Introduction, Acknowledgements

The City of Leicester has a long history pre-dating the Roman Conquest, evidenced by the Jewry Wall and other surviving remains of that period. It has strong connections with Simon de Montfort (1208-1265) who was instrumental in establishing the first English parliament, held in Leicester Castle. King Richard III passed through Leicester in 1485 on his way to Bosworth Field, while Cardinal Wolsey (c1475-1530) is one of the most familiar figures connected with historic Leicester. The Earls of Leicester, especially Robert Dudley, had strong associations with Queen Elizabeth I. In the Nineteenth Century Leicester developed into an industrial centre renowned for its footwear and hosiery industries while in the Twentieth Century engineering became well established. All combined to create the general wealth of the city and its inhabitants, who had some protection against economic depression, particularly in the early 1930s. Leicester became famous as the home of Freeman Hardy & Willis Shoes, Byfords & Wolsey Knitwear and Corahs, a major producer of fashion goods whose own trade mark was 'St Margaret' and who supplied Marks & Spencer under the 'St Michael' brand name. For decades the Leicester-made Imperial typewriter was an essential item of equipment in offices throughout the land. Yet Leicester, its past history and more recent industrial fame does not appear to have received the recognition due. The same could be said of its municipally owned public transport system, so highly regarded until the imposition of deregulation.

From 1904 until 1949 Leicester was served by the most outstanding medium sized tramway system (it became part of Leicester City Transport after 1935) in the country. It was owned by the Corporation itself and controlled by Councillors elected to the Transport Committee. These were men of the highest calibre, as were the successive General Managers and Engineers. The overall quality of the tramcars, equipment and buildings was unsurpassed and they survived for forty-five years until replacement by the diesel bus.

Over thirty years have elapsed since the publication of the very comprehensive though sadly long out of print *Leicester's Trams in Retrospect* by the late Mark Pearson. This book is not intended to rival that definitive history but is a timely reminder of an efficient and environmentally friendly form of public transport which until the end of the 1939-45 War was providing 60% of the services available, with attractive well-maintained tramcars. The service frequency provided on all the main routes is now unheard of in the 21st Century. Photographic credits are stated wherever known and I acknowledge with gratitude many of the prints provided by Peter Newland from his own collection and also particularly Glynn Wilton, the photographic archivist at the National Tramway Museum, Crich, Derbyshire where the sole surviving Leicester Tram No.76 is displayed in the main exhibition hall. The reader will find a visit to the Museum well worthwhile, not only to see Leicester's No.76 but to experience a ride on the many working trams amid the Derbyshire countryside. Many of the photographs have not as far as I am aware been published before and have been carefully chosen to remind us of Leicester in the electric tramway era. The *Leicester Mercury* has been most helpful by granting permission to reproduce some photographs previously used in their own publications.

I would like to acknowledge the publishers, Irwell Press to whom credit is due for their confidence in my ability to compile this book to their exacting standards.

Finally, this book would not have been possible without the encouragement and help of my son, Martin and the tolerance of my wife and daughter.

The Midland Railway station and London Road about 1920, and covered top tram No.124 approaches on a Clarendon Park via London Road service. The open top tram displaying an advert for the Palace Theatre in Belgrave Gate is on a circular service to Melbourne Road via Humberstone Road – the first route to close, on 13 December 1933. The station façade, designed by C. Trubshaw, is the only building in this post card view still standing, eighty years later; the station itself is now the only one in the city, serving London St Pancras and, to the north, Nottingham, Derby and Sheffield.

An early, 1905, view of tram No.65, noteworthy for depicting the original open top condition of the tramcars. This was typical of all of the early cars as delivered. The overhead wires in London Road, outside the Midland station, are supported by ornate iron gantries – later removed when motorised traffic increased. Photograph Peter Newland Collection.

A period post card of Granby Street about 1930. Tram No.117 approaches the junction with Rutland Street and Belvoir Street, where a traffic policeman stands on a discarded wooden fruit and veg box between the running lines. Saxone on the left and Dolcis next to the Wellington Hotel were once familiar shoe retailers throughout the British Isles. The 'Evening Mail' placard reads *'Test Match … Latest Score…'* We shudder…

A splendid early 1930s view of the LMS station on London Road, dating from 1892 and now a superbly restored listed building. The then modern building behind was originally occupied by the Inland Revenue who let shops at street level to a variety of traders. In this scene tram No.66 heads towards the city centre and then to Narborough Road. In the opposite direction car No.147, destined for East Park Road, loads passengers awaiting on the central reservation. The time is 5.15pm and the shadows are lengthening, although the rush hour has yet to begin – most workers did not leave their shops and offices until 5.30pm.

In early 1939 tram No.84, an early repaint in the modified livery introduced in 1937 is on a Route 1 service to Western Park. It will load its passengers at the High Street loading bay opposite Lloyds Bank. At a time when the public were exhorted to 'Buy British' at least three foreign vehicles can be found in this picture – two American Hudson Terraplanes and an Opel 'Kadett' a German import – maybe an imprudent purchase in view of the imminent war against Germany. Today the scene is unrecognisable, for virtually all the buildings have been demolished to make way for the Haymarket Centre.

This busy scene at the Clock Tower dates from 1906. There are three trams on the north-south running lines (certainly not 'keeping left') while a further two trams are in Eastgate. Not all the trams are identifiable but the covered top car would have been from the 1905 batch (Nos.101-120). No.36, destined for Belgrave, is one of the original batch delivered in 1904 for the opening of the system, as is No.16 (en route to Fosse Road according to the destination blind). In the background No.45 displaying an advert for the Palace Theatre has just passed a drinking house prominently advertising McConnells old Irish Whiskey. This was The Eclipse pub in the 1940s and 1950s. Pearsons at No.1 Cheapside had become 'Corts Ltd' a renowned hardware shop, while the Leicester Coffee House was to become a branch of 'Burtons the Tailor'. All three establishments can be found in different form elsewhere in this account of Leicester's trams.

A Brief Overview

1. The Rise of Leicester's Tram System

On Christmas Eve 1874 the horse drawn tramway era began in Leicester when a second-hand vehicle (one of six bought, unlikely enough, from Islington and Camberwell Corporation in London) traversed the newly laid track from the Clock Tower to Belgrave, terminating at the Folly Inn. It was operated by the 'Leicester Tramways Company Limited' formed in 1872 by a Mr Busby of Liverpool and a Mr Turton of Leeds to construct tram lines on London Road, Humberstone Road and Belgrave Road using the standard gauge of 4ft. 8½in. The narrow gauge of 3ft. 6in. was considered impractical by the promoters.

It had been eleven years earlier, however, that Solomon Andrews, a forward looking and successful businessman, had given the inhabitants of Leicester their first taste of public transport. In 1863 he had introduced a horse bus service which ran along Belgrave Road through the town centre and up London Road.

The Leicester Tramways Company Ltd. obtained the requisite powers under the Leicester Tramways Order (1873) to operate their system in conjunction with certain financial and operational agreements with the Corporation. Belgrave Road was the first operational line, followed by Humberstone Road in March 1875 and London Road on 14 August 1875. From 27 March 1876 a Hughes Patent Steam Tramway engine ran experimentally on the Belgrave route. The experiment was not considered successful and the engine was taken away to Govan, Glasgow after a short period.

In 1877 an Act of Parliament was obtained for the purpose of reconstituting the original company and extending the sphere of operation to Aylestone; this opened on 7 June 1878, followed by the Churchgate line on 29 August 1878. The revised Share Capital was fixed at £100,000 and the loan capital at £24,000.

The tramway and bus operations, both still horse powered, operated in competition with each other until 1888 when the tramway company (concerned about the threat the horse buses presented) organised a take-over of the horse bus system. They bought out the good Solomon Andrews for £8,000 which among other things covered the acquisition of thirteen horse buses and 78 horses, together with stables and buildings in Thurcaston Road. The tram company, its faith still firmly with the horse, prospered and at its peak in 1886 had a fleet of 46 trams working its five routes – which, by all historical accounts, were financially successful.

In June 1901 Leicester Corporation exercised their rights to buy out the privately owned tramway company upon the expiry of the lease, paying a total of £134,110 for 39 trams, 30 buses, 375 horses, nine miles of track and all the associated buildings and equipment. Radical change was very much in the air and as early as November 1900 a sub-committee of the new Tramways Department had compiled a report looking at every conceivable 'Method of Propulsion' for the tramways. The most cost-effective, it was determined, was an electrified overhead wire system. Yet the Town Council (Leicester was not a city until 1919) was against the use of overhead wires, particularly on aesthetic grounds. Unable to decide, they sought the advice of Mr E. Manville, a consultant engineer who came to the same conclusion as the original sub-committee. There were continued reservations from some members of the council but the alternative of a sub-

The original ornate overhead wire standards in the centre of London Road, about 1908. Perceived to be a traffic hazard as the number of vehicles increased, they were removed after the Great War. Open top car No.2 carrying a Bovril advert is heading for the Clock Tower and then Melton Road; it is about to pass top covered tram No.107, climbing uphill on a service to East Park Road.

Gallowtree Gate, from the top floor of the National Provincial Bank on the corner of Horsefair Street. Tram No.112, one of the original twenty top covered cars built in 1905 by Dick Kerr & Co of Preston, heads towards the Clock Tower on a Melbourne Road circular service. W.H. Newman Ltd were a long-established tobacconists who traded from the same premises for many years. The Liverpool Victoria Friendly Society has thrived and is a well-regarded insurance company even today. Sticklands Wool Depot & Lloyd Bros. Artificial Teeth have long ceased to trade and the buildings on the right of the picture have been either demolished or much altered.

merged conduit method of collection would, it was found, have cost in excess of £1,000,000 against the expected £650,000 for an overhead trolley system. It was these cost differences that finally led to the adoption of the latter.

After much deliberation, reconstruction of the tramways using electric pro-pulsion by an overhead trolley system ('of exceptional neatness', according to *The Tramway and Railway World* of 9 June 1904) took place in the period 1902-1904. The new permanent way, including the complex layout around the Clock Tower which formed the hub of the system was laid by the Corporation's own staff under the supervision of the Borough Surveyor and Tramways Engi-neer, Mr E.G. Mawbey. The existing trackwork for the horse tram routes was too light for the new electric system so replacements were required. The new track was supplied by Hadfields Lim-ited of Sheffield. The outstanding qual-

In 1905 open top tram No.74 (built 1904) heads out of town to Clarendon Park having just passed the Midland Bank on the corner of Bishop Street – at one time the largest provincial branch of the bank. The Wellington Hotel was open for business on the right-hand corner of Rutland Street. Barrows pushed by boys make up the only traffic on the road.

A post card view showing open top car No.127 at Belgrave outside the Champion Hotel in Loughborough Road, shortly after inauguration of the trams. The tram is heading to the Clock Tower and then East Park Road. Frys Chocolate was sold from the shop to the left of the pony and trap. To the right on the corner of Belgrave Street is an off licence which sold Allsops beers and on the wall is a sign giving details of Great Central Railway services. This post card was posted in August 1906 to a Miss Winn at Ivy House, New Bolingbroke, Boston Lincs, with the message *'Having a fine time. It is like home to be in Leicester again. Hoping you will like this view'*.

ity of the work undertaken was noted in the technical press, particularly the contemporary trade journal *Tramway and Railway World*.

Power for the new system was generated at the new LERO (I have never yet found what LERO means!) power station in Painter Street, which was owned by the Tramways Department. In December 1919 ownership of this power station was transferred to the City Electricity Department, by order of the council.

Trials of the new electric trams took place on 21 April 1904 when No.20 ran to Belgrave. The 'Electric Era' proper commenced a few weeks later on 18 May 1904. After a 2pm reception at the Town Hall the 300 guests were conveyed in twelve horse trams for Painter Street where Mrs Flint, wife of the then Chairman of the Tramways Committee and Mrs Smith, wife of the Vice Chairman, officially switched the power on. The party made a ceremonial tour of Belgrave and Stoneygate in three decorated trams. There then followed the customary tea, speeches and presentations. Tram No.3 conveyed the Mayor, Councillors and tramway officials to Stoneygate and back on the inaugural run.

The system was opened to the public that evening, 18 May 1904 at 7pm. Such was the interest and enthusiasm for the new trams that every one was packed solid with eager passengers until the last service at 11pm that night. *The Tramway and Railway World* called

Leicester's tramways 'as good an example of a trolley line as can be found in this country'.

The new electric system encompassed routes to Stoneygate, Belgrave, Clarendon Park (via London Road) and Melbourne Road. The latter was circular, running via Humberstone Road and London Road. The system was further expanded with the addition of routes to Narborough Road, Western Park and Fosse Road on 12 July 1904. The route to Aylestone commenced operation on 5 September 1904 and incorporated a short siding near to the Rugby Football Ground for stabling trams on match day special duties. The next stage of growth saw the extension of the Humberstone Road route to a new terminus at Humberstone Drive, together with a new route along East Park Road, a few weeks later on 1 November 1904. The final extension of 1904 was the Groby Road route opened on 22 December; the last new route of this period opened on 8 June 1905, to Melton Road.

The tramways proved extremely popular with the public and were financially very successful; the major routes radiated out from the Clock Tower, and made it the most important part of the system. Traffic grew from 25,890,030 passengers carried in 1905 to 37,914,773 in 1914. The trams covered 4,137,262 miles and income generated amounted to £149,664 for the year. An annual net surplus of between £15-20,000 was normal at that time. During the First World War there was

an enormous growth in passengers carried, putting the system under great strain as maintenance declined due to lack of both materials and manpower. One authorised extension opened however, on 20 September 1915, running to Fosse Road via King Richard's Road.

The lack of maintenance during the 1914-1918 war contributed to the poor state of the tramway system and on the cessation of hostilities a programme of maintenance and renewal was rapidly put into operation. In 1919 62,434,056 passengers were carried which stands as a record, an even more impressive one given the shortage of staff and materials.

After World War I the next extension of the system was the line to Clarendon Park via Welford Road, opened on 26 September 1922. This line involved the steep climb up Cemetery Hill which required fifteen trams to be equipped with slipper brakes as an additional safety measure for the descent of the hill. The last extensions were laid on railway sleepers purchased from the Great Central Railway. Of these, the Blackbird Road line was built specifically for the Royal Agricultural Show and ran on a central reservation separate from the road. Beginning operation on 27 June 1924, it also served the new bakery of Frears and Blacks together with many new factories erected along the route in the post-war expansion of manufacturing in the city.

During the period 1921-1930 the tramway 'infrastructure', if we can ap-

At the end of the First World War tram No.132 on an East Park Road working heads toward the Clock Tower, passing the Palace Theatre and the Floral Hall – later a cinema which in its final years acquired a 'reputation' for the *risqué* films shown. W. Billson Son & Co. were well known tent and marquee manufacturers while the South Knighton Dye Works and Laundry has recently been demolished. Tram No.132 was involved in a serious collision in 1915 but was repaired. The delivery vehicle BC539 is a Model T Ford.

Four brand new trams on display but not in the tropics – the palm trees are in pots. The location is the rather less exotic Abbey Park Road, the leading car No.45 displaying 'Belgrave' as its destination. The advert for Simpkin & James is a reminder of the renowned provisions merchants whose main premises were in Horsefair Street and Market Place and where all the more exclusive produce could be obtained. When the shop closed, it was the passing of an era. The trading name was retained by the excellent wine and spirits shop in Cank Street – still owned by two former employees.

A poor old folded post card, but a valuable record. During the 1914-1918 Great War, lady conductors were employed to replace men called up for military service. In this post card view of tram No.139 taken in St Barnabas Road the lady conductress and her driver have their picture taken. For a lesson in social evolution and the Final Triumph of women, compare our Great War 'clippie' with her 1949 successor on page 24 . None of the products advertised on the tram are now on the market and the trams ceased to run past the Palace Theatre when the system closed in November 1949. The theatre itself was demolished in the 1960s.

ply the modern term, was improved and automatic trolley reversers were installed at every terminus. These were simple triangles of overhead wires enabling the car to reverse out on a sort of 'V' and run forward to point the right way for its return. The trolley followed the cable to its maximum extent and back as the tram changed tracks. In High Street the track opposite Lloyds Bank was realigned and a kerbside loading barrier installed for routes to the western districts of the city. A similar alteration took place in Bowling Green Street for the Aylestone and Clarendon Park (via Welford Road) services. A central loading shelter was erected in Humberstone Gate for the benefit of passengers for Coleman Road and Humberstone. A number of minor improvements continued to be made to ensure that, unlike neighbouring towns and cities, Leicester continued to be served by a well-maintained fleet of tramcars, providing an unsurpassed level of service. The Coleman Road Route opened on 31 March 1927 and was destined to be the final addition to the system; sadly it had the shortest life, closing only eleven years later.

Until 13 December 1933 when the Melbourne Road Route closed, at its maximum extent the total route mileage of the Leicester City Tramways was 22 miles, 7 furlongs and 126 yards. They had been Leicester Corporation Tramways until 1919 and from 1935, recognising the increasing importance of buses, had been renamed Leicester City Transport. On most of the system, the tram tracks ran in the streets, the exception to this being Blackbird Road and Coleman Road which ran on central reservations. The greater part of the system was double track although some single track with passing loops existed on the Clarendon Park, East Park Road and Fosse Road Routes.

ITS DAYS' WORK DONE.

From Christmas Eve 1874 until October 1904, horsedrawn trams plied the streets of Leicester. This picture of horse tram No.38 was taken on a farm at Barkby, Leicestershire where, after withdrawal, it was used as a summerhouse.

Tram No.101 was the first covered top vehicle to be delivered to the Corporation and appears to be almost new in this view at Belgrave Terminus as the crew pose for their portrait. Note the two schoolboys seated on the upper deck at the top of the stairs.

A Brief Overview
2. The Tramcars

In June 1903, in anticipation of the new electric working, two sample trams were delivered, No.1 from Dick Kerr & Co, Preston and No.2 from Brush, Loughborough. While No.2 cost a little less than No.1 (£497 18s against £510) the council preferred the product of Dick Kerr & Co. Brush had made their car to the council's specification but Dick Kerr had incorporated a number of additional refinements. After much negotiation and indeed acrimony with Brush the contract for the original batch of a total of 58 open top Tramcars was awarded to Dick Kerr. No.2 was returned to Brush and subsequently found service in the London Metropolitan fleet as No.191.

The chosen livery became Crimson Lake and Cream with over ten coats of primer before the application of the colours and varnish. With an elaborate lining out in gold leaf, the appearance and quality of the new trams was considered to be unsurpassed. The bodywork incorporated oak, ash, mahogany and maple.

The cars had seating for 22 passengers downstairs and 34 upstairs, in the form of longitudinal wooden benching downstairs and cross benching upstairs. 'Up top' the seats were also wooden but with backs which flipped over according to the direction of travel.

A new purpose-built Tram Depot and workshops was constructed in Abbey Park Road in 1903. A total of 153 trams could be housed in the depot and the arrangements were accordingly comprehensive. These were improved in 1915 with further workshop facilities, enabling the corporation to erect new trams 'in house'. In the course of time the stables and shed at New Parks, which had been used for the horse drawn vehicles, were sold. The old horse trams too were sold off and at least one was known to have ended its life on a farm at Barkby Thorpe.

The original electric tram routes were successful from the first and as the system expanded the original fleet of 59 trams (the 58 from Dick Kerr plus the sample No.1) had to be increased. A further forty vehicles, constructed once again by the preferred manufacturer Dick Kerr at Preston were delivered later in that first year of operation, 1904. At the same time a single deck water car for maintenance purposes was delivered and took the number 100. (The cars themselves were by now numbered 1-99). The next delivery of new trams were Nos.101-121, ordered in 1905 from the United Electric Car Company of Preston – successors to Dick Kerr. Trams in this batch, unlike the earlier one, were fitted with upper deck covers. These later required modification to provide improved ventilation in the roof. A further twenty cars, Nos.122-141 built as open top cars to the original design, were acquired later in the same year (1905) from the same supplier, together with an additional water car. This batch, except No.137, had roofs by 1912. This car was renumbered 100; tram 141 became 137 and water car 100 assumed fleet No.141 for a few months only. The Tramways Department built a third water car in 1909 from a kit of parts supplied by the original manufacturer. The water cars were frequently renumbered and eventually became 179-181.

By 1912 the tram fleet consisted of 100 open top cars, Nos.1-100, 20 canopy roof cars Nos.101-120 and twenty stand-

During the early 1930s Belgrave Gate was widened and the original interlaced track, by then in woebegone condition, was removed and replaced by normal track as seen here. Tram No.118 is approaching on the new track and will pass The General House Furnishers and The Griffin Inn. Hansons still exist as an independent brewery, producing excellent beers in the North Midlands, but they sold this pub in the early 1990s.

ard roof cars Nos.121-140 together with the water vehicles. The next to be ordered featured a longer wheelbase of 7ft 0in (against 6ft of the earlier cars) to allow for longer entrance platforms designed for 'Pay As You Enter ('PAYE') operation. These cars assumed the running sequences 141-150. The PAYE scheme was confined initially to the Stoneygate and Narborough Road routes and after fifteen months was discontinued.

Immediately prior to the outbreak of World War I in 1914 the Tramways Department took the decision to convert all open top trams to covered top, using the improved roof design from the manufacturers – UEC Co.

Cars 141-150, boasting an increased capacity of 60 passengers were delivered from Preston in 1913 and in the following year ten further cars came, from Brush. By this time the acrimony between the Corporation and the firm had been forgotten and this order for ten new long wheelbase trams, Nos.151-160, went to the Loughborough manufacturer.

The growth of traffic and impending extensions to Clarendon Park via Welford Road in 1922 presaged the need for yet more tramcars. In anticipation of this and other proposed extensions the Tramways Department constructed Nos.161-166 itself, from components supplied by the United Electric Company. UEC also secured the final order for twelve cars, Nos.167-178. Top cover for all cars was standard by now and they saw a reversion back to the shorter 6ft wheelbase. Such was the success of the original design that sixteen years later it was still considered suitable for the final trams being built. The Leicester City Tramways fleet totalled at its peak 178 cars, together with three water cars.

All tramcars and the three maintenance/water cars had Brill 21E four wheeled trucks and 'Standardised Electrical Equipment' comprising 25hp electric motors supplied by Dick Kerr. Over the years many cars were fitted with more powerful 40hp motors. Some also received equipment supplied by Metropolitan Vickers and others got equipment from the British Thompson Houston Co (BTH).

Additionally there were three petrol driven overhead wire maintenance lorries. The original Leyland Lorry delivered in 1911 (registration BC 1078) has been preserved and is believed to be the oldest Leyland vehicle in existence. Two additional Leyland vehicles were delivered in 1924 and were of equally antiquated appearance, with solid tyres. Both survived, unlikely enough, until they were scrapped in 1950, after the closure of the system and removal of all overhead equipment.

While most of the cars were stabled at the Abbey Park Road Depot, there were two small district depots, at Stoneygate and Narborough Road, housing six trams each. These were taken out of use in 1922 when the former permanent way stores in Humberstone Gate (which had a narrow entrance – 'the hole in the wall' – adjacent to the Bell Hotel) were adapted to accommodate twenty-five trams, specifically for use at peak travel times.

As no alternative mode of public transport existed in Leicester before 1924 the Tramway reigned supreme and a programme of modernisation and improvements for the benefit of passengers and staff alike was put in hand from 1921. The drivers demanded more protection from the elements and so No.86, an original open top car, was completely rebuilt as the first experimen-

Above. By the time this photograph was taken about 1906, trams were well established as the way to travel in Leicester. Nos.8 and 26 from the original batch delivered by Dick Kerr/Preston in 1904 are both operating the Melbourne Road circular route but in opposite directions. Kemp the Jewellers and Newmans tobacconists were well established businesses, both trading from the same shops for several decades.

Left. Horsebuses were introduced in Leicester in 1863 by Solomon Andrews. No.7 is depicted in 1892 near the 'Hygienic Bakery' in Braunstone Gate. Two ladies on the upper deck have umbrellas raised(!) to protect themselves from the sun. Photograph Les Orton/ Peter Newland Collection.

tal fully enclosed car and re-equipped with powerful motors supplied by BTH. While the concept was a success, the cost of extending this sort of cover to the whole fleet was prohibitive and so a less elaborate and aesthetically more attractive solution was achieved, through the simple expedient of enclosing the upper balcony and lower platform with an effective standard screen. This evolution of Leicester's trams from open top to a standard all-enclosed appearance took over nineteen years, six cars being withdrawn from traffic before they could be so modernised.

Eleven cars were fitted with a revised arrangement of transverse upholstered leather seats on the lower decks only. Two further tramcars were so fitted on both decks. The installation of route number blinds throughout the fleet was undertaken from 1932 onwards.

In 1937 a new simplified livery was introduced. The trams were repainted in maroon, with only the window frames and a narrow band around the base of the body being in cream, by way of relief. Under the windows a narrow orange line separated the two colours. The trams now had a modern appearance although no structural alterations had been made. At the same time provision was made for additional route information to be displayed on wooden boards mounted outside, underneath the lower deck windows, 9ft long and 5in. deep. This was promptly abandoned on the outbreak of war in September 1939.

Twenty-three trams were fitted with extended lower deck frames between 1930 and 1937 to allow enlarged platforms to be fitted and to improve passenger comfort. This was destined to be the final improvement in the development of Leicester's Tramcars.

The 'Hole in the Wall' between the Bell Hotel and the Transport Enquiry offices in Humberstone Gate. No.16 (ex-No.108) is entering this Central Depot in September 1949, having finished duty on the Belgrave route for nearly the last time, as closure was imminent. Only the lady on the left glances at the scene, with other passers-by oblivious that the tramway era was almost at an end. Photograph F.N.T. L.L. Jones.

A Brief Overview
3. The Decline

Motor buses first appeared in 1924 and after the final tram extension (Coleman Road in 1927) were used when new public transport routes were introduced. The cost of tramway extensions had become prohibitive by comparison.

By 1933 the Melbourne Road tram route was worn out and rather than renew the line (which was mainly single track with passing loops) it was decided to replace the trams with buses. This first route closure also saw the first withdrawal – the six cars which had never been modernised. Though 'withdrawn', some were used occasionally on special workings until 1937, when they were finally dismantled.

By 1937 lengthy debates were taking place as to the future of public transport in Leicester, as in many municipalities throughout the country – the tram was being consigned to history. The Leicester system, however, was still in an excellent state of repair and, crucially, was profitable. Moreover it provided an efficient and frequent service on all routes. A report compiled by the then General Manager, Mr Ben England concluded that trams should be replaced *gradually* with the chosen successor being the diesel bus. One of the

fundamental issues affecting the running of the Leicester tram system was that the City Electricity Department had a monopoly as the power provider and had been consistently overcharging the Tramways, thus distorting the financial returns. The Tramways management were understandably piqued – hence the recommendation for diesel buses rather than electrically powered trolley buses.

Two more closures took place before the Second World War broke out in 1939. Coleman Road closed on 23 October 1938 (superseded by a bus route which served new housing estates) and King Richard's Road followed on 2 April 1939. It was a duplicate and unnecessary line by-passed by the Hinckley Road route to Western Park. The closure also led to the withdrawal of a further fourteen cars, although three were subsequently reconditioned and returned to service on the outbreak of War, leaving a fleet of 161 trams to cater for the immense increase in traffic that was to come as a consequence of the War. Only one tram, No.19, was withdrawn during the war years and that as a result of accident damage in 1941. The engineers, both electrical and mechanical, had to contend with a lack of spares

and items necessary to maintain the fleet in full working order yet by resorting to basic skills and improvisation they succeeded gallantly. The 160 trams managed to carry around 45 million passengers per annum during the years 1939-1945, providing 60% of the public transport service. Wartime also restricted the use of buses, through fuel shortage and rationing. The buses were frequently limited merely to feeder services for the trams.

After 1936 Leicester had been the last East Midlands municipality to retain a tram system – how fortunate that decision in 1937 not to abandon the system in haste was to prove!

At the end of World War Two the Clarendon Park via Welford Road route was closed, on 1 May 1945. It was a little-used line duplicated in any event by a bus service which ran to Knighton Lane. The track was retrieved and used in essential repairs in other parts of the city, new track being unobtainable in the aftermath of World War Two. The Tramway system was still providing 60% of all public transport in the city but the lack of maintenance in the war years combined with age of the trams (many of them now over forty years old) hastened the system's demise, in No-

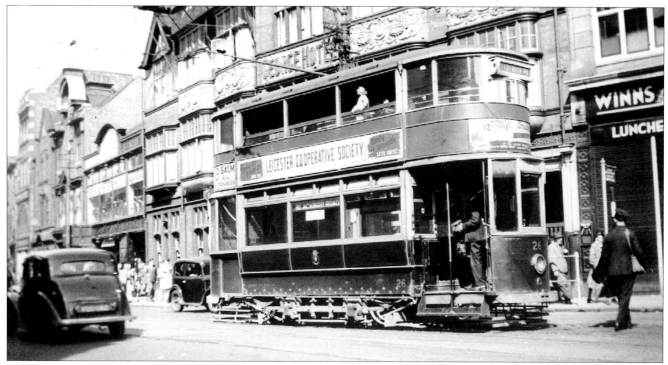

Tram No.26, originally built by Dick Kerr of Preston in 1904 as an open top vehicle, on 26 May 1947. It is basking in the sun outside the George Hotel in the Haymarket; it was rebuilt and modernised in the period 1931-1937 with extended frames – identified by the double lines of rivets at the body base. The platforms were enlarged to lengthen the lower deck and improve passenger loading and unloading. More powerful motors were fitted to many of the trams during their lives, but with the exception of No.86 (the experimental rebuild) the remainder of the fleet had a pleasingly uniform external appearance. An Austin 7 'Ruby' of 1935 vintage is squeezing between the tram and the kerbside outside 'The George' while a Standard '14' heads down into Belgrave Gate from the Haymarket. At this date most of the Leicester Tramway system was still open, carrying 45 million passengers per year. The whole area is now part of the Haymarket Centre. Photograph National Tramway Museum, M.J. O'Connor

Melton Road terminus in 1948, with No.38 parked by the time clock awaiting departure for Humberstone – Route 8. The shadow in the roadway is cast by the 'Premier Works' a building which still exists. The houses too, still stand but all have been converted into small offices or restaurants providing oriental and Asian cuisine. In this picture not a car is in sight, for a ration of one gallon of petrol, and poor quality to boot, did not go far. It was marketed as 'POOL' petrol, indicating that all the well-known petrol companies such as Shell, BP and the rest 'pooled' their production with the limited output distributed under government control. Photograph National Tramway Museum, M.J. O'Connor.

The former small tram depot at Stoneygate built to accommodate six trams closed in 1922. Thereafter it became the 'Terminus Garage' and hand operated petrol pumps were installed on the pavement at right angles to the road. H.A. Browett Ltd., for many years the main dealers for Standard cars in Leicester, rented the property from the Corporation and garaged cars inside the building. During the early 1970s it was used as a railway museum housing several historic locomotives including the Midland Railway 'Spinner' No.673 now on display at Butterley, Derby. In May 2000 the building still appears to be structurally sound, though disused. Photo G. Creese.

vember 1949. By that time a fleet of 160 new buses had been acquired to replace the tramcars.

The first major post-war route closure was that of Aylestone Road which ceased to operate on 5 January 1947. This was a logical move as it enabled the track in Horsefair Street (used only for access to and from the main depot in Abbey Park Road) to be recovered and used elsewhere. A batch of early post-war buses was acquired to replace the trams on this route.

With the closure of the Fosse Road route on 15 July 1947, withdrawal and scrapping of trams began in earnest, with at least twenty-nine cars being withdrawn. Some tram bodies were sold including that of No.76, which would eventually be preserved.

The remnants of the system soldiered on as closures accelerated; on 21 November 1948 the Narborough Road and Western Park (Hinckley Road) routes were converted to bus operation. This led to the next wave of tramcar withdrawals, with eighteen being taken out of service.

The system now had less than a year of life left as more new buses became available and the trams were given minimal maintenance and cleaning. Nevertheless in the final year of operation, 1948-1949, an operational fleet of just 72 trams carried over 40 million passengers.

On 23 January 1949 the very last tram ran, to Groby Road, followed by the closure of the line to Clarendon Park on 13 March 1949, East Park Road on 15 May 1949 and Melton Road on 3 July.

The 'Last Tram', No.58, at Humberstone Terminus on 9 November 1949, on its final working back to the Clock Tower with civic dignitaries and transport officials aboard. It had been highly decorated for the occasion with the civic coat of arms applied at both cab ends. On the lower deck the panelling reads 'AFTER MUCH BINDING –THESE YOU HAVE LOVED ARE NOW BANNED WAGONS. BUSES TAKE IT FROM HERE'. Obscure now, these were references to popular radio programmes of the period. On the other side was a more poignant message:

'We mourn the loss of faithful friends
from the streets of our grand old city
To move with the times we cannot have lines
So – go they must – it's a pity'.

Between 18 May 1904 and 9 November 1949, the trams covered 171,802,000 miles and carried 2,068,450,000 passengers. It wasn't bad! This tram went to the breaker's yard along with the final survivors. One tram, No.36, was reputedly set aside for preservation by Leicester Museum as it was in above average condition. However the committee responsible for deciding its fate took its time and did not come to a decision until a meeting on 25 April 1950. Procrastination being the thief of time – it was too late. No.36 had been broken up only the day before, 24 April, at Abbey Park Road Depot and the unique opportunity lost. Fifty years ago it seemingly mattered not. Luckily No.76 was discovered in 1960 in use as a cricket pavilion in Yorkshire. Beautifully restored it can be seen today at the National Tramway Museum at Crich, Derbyshire.

This left the lines to Stoneygate, Belgrave and Humberstone as the surviving routes; just 36 trams survived to maintain these services.

On 9 October the sole cross-city routes, Stoneygate and Belgrave were closed and the end was in sight; fifteen cars now remained to serve the last route, No.8, to Humberstone.

On a very wet and dismal day, 9 November 1949, the final services ran to Humberstone, eight trams being used until at 3.30pm the last trip from the city centre was made by car No.58, highly decorated for the occasion. As on the opening day in May 1904, the final tram carried civic dignitaries and senior transport department officials who witnessed the end of the most successful and longest-lived medium sized tramway in the country. No.58 entered the Abbey Park Road Depot at 16.10pm and the power supply was switched off for ever. Between 18 May 1904 and 9 November 1949 the trams had run 171.8

million miles and carried over two *billion* passengers. The surplus revenues generated had been apportioned to relieve the burden on the rate payers for many years. It was not *quite* the end as the trucks and underframes of approximately twenty cars were sold for service to the Calcutta Tramways Company Limited of India.

As mentioned earlier some of the bodies were sold privately for other uses. In 1960 a few enthusiasts found the mortal remains of tram No.76 (withdrawn in 1947) in use as a cricket pavilion at East Cowick near Goole, Yorkshire.

It was purchased for £100 and removed to Crich near Matlock in Derbyshire at what is now the National Tramway Museum. No.76 was painstakingly restored by a small group of volunteers over a nine year period to the condition and livery in which it ran in 1920. Now the centre piece of a static display in the main exhibition hall, it is

a fitting and priceless survivor of Leicester's Tramway heritage.

Bibliography

Leicester Trams by K.W. Smith published by the Light Railway Transport League (London Area) Second Edition 1964.
Leicester's Trams in Retrospect by M.S.W. Pearson published by Tramway Publications, National Tramway Museum 1970.
Tramcars in Leicester by M.S.W Pearson published by Tramway Publications, National Tramway Museum 1988.
Tramway Society Bulletin Winter 1940 edition.
The City of Leicester Passenger Transport Official Handbook 1936.
City of Leicester Tramways Official Souvenir of the coming of age of the Electric Tramcar System 1925.
The official opening of the administrative offices – Leicester City Transport 1937.

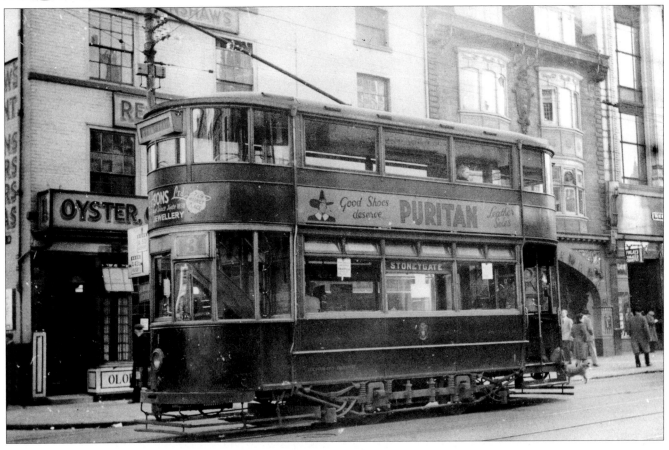

Above. Tram No.1, originally built by Dick Kerr of Preston early in 1904 as an open top car, about to depart for Stoneygate in December 1948, on Route 3. The advert, of course, is for footwear. This is the loading point in Humberstone Gate outside Olorenshaws Restaurant – famous for oysters and other seafood delicacies, which were much sought after in the post-war years of austerity. Tram No.1 is in its final condition and despite being almost 45 years old and nearing the end of its life, is still well cared for and respectably clean. Photograph National Tramway Museum.

Left. On 28 March 1941 tram No.19 was involved in a fatal accident in the blackout. The damage sustained was sufficient to warrant its withdrawal, although the upper deck and roof were salvaged as spares for the remainder of the fleet. It is seen here in the Abbey Park Depot yard. Photograph Peter Newland Collection.

The Clock Tower in Leicester's city centre and the focal point for nearly all the central tram services. This is May 1937, and High Street and Eastgates are decorated for the Coronation of King George VI and Queen Elizabeth. Leicester City Transport decorated every tram in service as demonstrated by this evocative picture of No.111 about to turn right into Gallowtree Gate, for Route 3 to Stoneygate. No.41 is approaching en route to Fosse Road, via Great Central Street – Dean and Dawson were booking agents for the London and North Eastern Railway and a number of shipping companies in the 1930s. No *Keep Left* rules existed for the trams at the Clock Tower – the track (see below) layout was one of the most complex in Britain. Photograph S.G. Jackman.

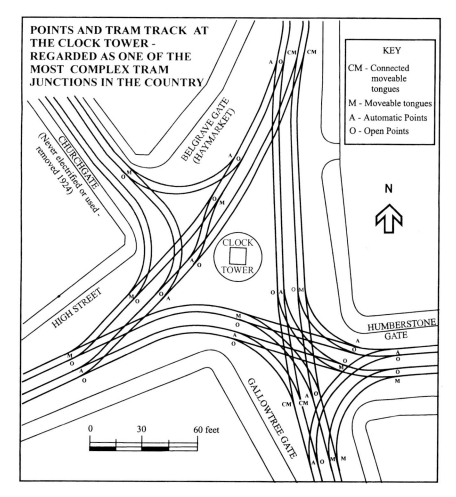

POINTS AND TRAM TRACK AT THE CLOCK TOWER - REGARDED AS ONE OF THE MOST COMPLEX TRAM JUNCTIONS IN THE COUNTRY

KEY

CM - Connected moveable tongues

M - Moveable tongues

A - Automatic Points

O - Open Points

CHURCHGATE (Never electrified or used - removed 1924)

BELGRAVE GATE (HAYMARKET)

CLOCK TOWER

HIGH STREET

N

HUMBERSTONE GATE

GALLOWTREE GATE

0   30   60 feet

In the 1930s Leicester City Tramways extended the platforms of twenty-three trams in order to strengthen the lower deck and improve the loading and unloading for passengers. No.136 was one of those so improved and modernised and in summer 1949 is about to leave Stoneygate Terminus for the Clock Tower; the conductress, stern authority personified, appears to have rung the bell while No.87 awaits its turn. The destination – Belgrave – confirms the date as this was the last remaining through tram route via the Clock Tower; it survived until 9 October 1949. Photograph National Tramway Museum.

On 10 August 1947 the experimental fully enclosed tram No.86 emerges from Abbey Park Road into Belgrave Road passing T.E.Cundy's decorator's shop. It is on a special enthusiasts' working which toured the Leicester tramway system, still largely intact at this date. No.86 was withdrawn in 1948, surviving as the unique rebuilt tram for twenty-five years. Road vehicles were thin on the ground at this time due to petrol rationing but this was also the Leicester Industrial Holiday and thousands of citizens were away at Skegness or Mablethorpe and other exotic resorts, making their way out of the city by train from Belgrave Road (ex-GNR) station opposite Cundy's Shop. Photograph National Tramway Museum.

August 1949 at Stoneygate Terminus. Trams Nos.66 and 89 (both extended platform rebuilds) await their turn to depart for the Clock Tower and onwards to Belgrave. On the left is a 'Gledhill' post-war time clock, mounted on a concrete base; the plate affixed to the pole gives the fare structure. It was 2½d to the Clock Tower, 2d to Victoria Park Gates and 1½d to Knighton Park Road. Together with a frequent service, the low fares ensured that the trams were always well patronised. Photograph National Tramway Museum.

Tram No.110 in September 1949, at the Stoneygate terminus. It was the last tram to retain the pre-1937 livery, the quality of which must have been exceptionally good as it is still presentable after more than twelve years' service. Photograph Leicestershire Museums.

Trackwork being laid at the junction of Horsefair Street, Granby Street and Gallowtree Gate about 1903. The workmen were Corporation employees, their white shirts seeming inappropriate to us today, given the arduous and dirty nature of the work. Dentists Bosworth and Fields occupied rooms in W.F. Johnson's building, and two doors away Lloyd Bros. (the two presumably had an arrangement) supplied artificial teeth to those who had lost their originals. Photograph National Tramway Museum.

The Stoneygate Terminus in August 1949. No.117 (to the right) is at the extremity of the line and about to reverse via the crossover. The automatic trolley reverser (a feature found at all Leicester tram termini) is clearly depicted – the overhead wiring was arranged in an equilateral triangle, and as the car reversed to cross the running lines the trolley pole would follow the overhead triangle to turn through 180 degrees. In this fashion it would be correctly positioned for the return journey. Meanwhile No.130 (the nearest tram) has also arrived, the two ladies appearing to have disembarked. The houses on the left are unaltered fifty years later while the road has been widened into a dual carriageway and junction for the Ring Road. The author spent many happy hours 'tramspotting' at this point, which is still a very pleasant location, even half a century on. Photograph National Tramway Museum.

On 18 August 1946 tram No.1 has just left the Blackbird Road reserved section and is about to pass under the former Great Central Railway (by now LNER) bridge on a Route 4 working to Clarendon Park via London Road. Some of the products advertised are still familiar today, such as Ovaltine and Domestos, while others have disappeared. Oxydol and *Picture Post* are no more and the railway itself has been dismantled, a victim of 1960s closures. The original concept of the Great Central was of a modern main line to connect with a projected Channel Tunnel. Whereas once we had a railway but no tunnel now the reverse applies and there is already talk of a revivified 'GC' thirty-odd years after we casually discarded the old one, built at such enormous cost in labour and treasure. Photograph National Tramway Museum.

Tram No.6 passes under the Fosse Road North railway bridge early in 1947. Castle's Motors advertise their Rootes Group dealership for Hillman Humber and Sunbeam Talbot cars, all marques now long consigned to history. The advertising hoardings are of interest. The Army needs ambitious men, while it is still demobilising wartime conscripts; Brooke Bond Tea is still very popular, while the Fosse Cinema was showing 'Calcutta' with Alan Ladd. The railway bridge has now been replaced by a footbridge. It once formed part of the Leicester & Swannington Railway – the terminus was at West Bridge. Photograph C. Carter.

Top left. The 'Hole in the Wall' between the City Transport Office and the Bell Hotel (that's the Public Bar on the right) in Humberstone Gate gave access to the Central Tram Depot, housing twenty-five trams for use at peak periods. No.16 was originally No.108, renumbered for some inexplicable reason on withdrawal of the original No.16, a 1904 car. On 15 Sept 1949 it is emerging for duty on Route 1, Belgrave, by then one of only three routes remaining. Closure was imminent and came on 9 October 1949. The tram is still in a presentable condition with clean windows, although its days were numbered.

Bottom left. On a foggy winter's day on 27 November 1945, No.13 is heading for Aylestone near the Leicester Rugby football ground. A Midland Red bus of 1932 vintage has some passengers on the L8 route. The tram carries an advert (lost in the mist) for the Kirby & West Dairy which has survived to the present day. The road has changed out of all recognition and is now part of a one way traffic system surrounding the Granby Halls and the football ground. Midland Red and Leicester City Transport no longer exist, both having been consumed by de-regulation and integration into other operators. Leicester City Transport is now 'First Bus'.

Below. Belvoir Street in 1946, and an early 1930s Daimler limousine leads a 1938 Ford 8 and an MG Midget – UT7490 dating from 1930, the young driver of which appears to be well aware of the close proximity of tram No.21, emerging from Bowling Green Street on a Route 5 working to Aylestone. Joseph Johnson's is now Fenwicks and as I write the only shop from this period to retain its identity is Young's Photographers. Cowling's Radio & Television shop has just closed, having traded for over sixty years from the same premises.

TRAMCAR SERVICES.			
THE AYLESTONE ROUTE.			
Aylestone Tramcars from either terminus every 4, 5 and 7 minutes.			
	Weekdays.	*Saturdays.*	*Sundays.*
First Car—Bowling Green St.	5.52 a.m.	5.52 a.m.	9.40 a.m.
,, ,, Terminus ..	6.10 a.m.	6.10 a.m.	9.58 a.m.
Last Car—Bowling Green St.	11. 0 p.m.	11.17 p.m.	10.46 p.m.
,, ,, Terminus ..	11.18 p.m.	11.35 p.m.	11. 4 p.m.

Above. On 7 July 1938 tram No.28 stands at the entrance to the original 1904 Tram Depot, resplendent in its original livery and bearing the legend Leicester City Tramways, indicating that it was repainted around 1934. Standing in Bay No.5, the destination – Melbourne Road – was by arrangement for the photographer, W.A. Camwell, as the route was the first to close, on 13 December 1933. The tramshed bays immediately to the right of this picture were destroyed by fire in August 1999 and several new buses were burnt out – the total cost of the damage was reported at several million pounds.

Top right. In the summer of 1947 tram No.30 is loaded to capacity on a circular working. On a fine day the upper deck windows are fully open to an extent that would give today's Health & Safety Commissars apoplexy! No passengers were ever known to have fallen 'overboard' during the entire lifetime of the system. No.30 appropriately carries an advert for 'Cephos' the physicians' remedy for headaches and so on and 'DDD Balm' for all skin troubles. The location is the Blackbird Road central reservation, opened 27 June 1924. Photograph I.R. Davidson.

TRAMCAR SERVICES.

NARBOROUGH ROAD ROUTE.

Narborough Road Tramcars from either Terminus every 3, 3½, 4, 4½, 5 and 6 minutes.

	Weekdays.	Saturdays.	Sundays.
First Car—Clock Tower ..	6.10 a.m.	6.10 a.m.	9.37½ a.m.
,, ,, Terminus ..	6.24 a.m.	6.24 a.m.	9.51½ a.m.
Last Car—Clock Tower ..	11.4½ p.m.	11.17 p.m.	10.46 p.m.
,, ,, Terminus ..	11.18½ p.m.	11.31 p.m.	11. 0 p.m.

Bottom right. In summer 1946, a very clean No.38 is on the Blackbird Road reservation, leaving a fare stage which announces a cost of 3d for the journey to the Clock Tower via Great Central Street. 'Yorkshire Relish' – 'the sauce of good taste' was extensively advertised on Leicester trams and enriched many an austere post-war meat dish. No.38 will cover six miles via the Clock Tower before reaching the Clarendon Park Terminus in Welford Road. The lone car is a 1938 Hillman Minx. Photograph A.D. Packer.

Melton Road terminus, in the summer of 1947. A number of passengers disembark, while the driver of No.38 waits to escort those who wish to cross the road. Two Tompkins Removal vans are emptying a typical 1930s semi-detached house which, incidentally, still exists.

No.58 was destined to be the final car to run in Leicester, on 9 November 1949. Some two years earlier it is halted by Grenfell Road, Stoneygate, awaiting clearance to the end of the line to set down the remaining passengers. It still shows some of the wartime white paint applied to the base of the bodywork. At this time Stoneygate was linked with the Fosse Road route – this closed on 15 July 1947. Photograph M.J. O'Connor.

15 September 1938, and No.47 is on the short Coleman Road route, closed on 23 October 1938, having been the last route to be opened in March 1927. Rapid housing development served by new bus services hastened its demise. Photograph courtesy Peter Newland.

BYYYY AND SAVE! (Translation: Be wise and save) Trams were used for many special occasions and on 11 March 1948 No.60 was so engaged at Groby Road Terminus, exhorting the citizens to hit a savings target of £400,000. A loud hailer was attached to attract attention and possibly clerks from the Post Office and the Leicester Trustee Savings Bank were aboard to do business. Photograph courtesy Peter Newland.

On a dull summer's day in 1938 No.61, rebuilt with extended platforms, pauses at the Stoneygate Terminus. It is in the old livery and would have been repainted about three years earlier. It carries the supplementary destination boards – nine feet long by five inches deep held in place by brackets outside the lower deck windows and painted in distinctive colours to represent each service. While the intention was good, in practice passengers were confused and it was discontinued on the outbreak of war. The houses behind No.61 in Grenfell Road are unchanged and the area is still a well regarded residential locality, sixty two years on. Photograph National Tramway Museum, H.B. Priestley.

Accidents will happen, but do not hit a tram! The Bedford lorry owned by Pickfords is in a sorry state after colliding with No.71 on 29 July 1943 at the Holden Street/Loughborough Road junction. A Transport Inspector wearing the regulation cap takes notes (left of picture) and onlookers, as always, gawp at the damage. No.71 sustained little hurt and remained in service until September 1949, still in its c.1934 livery. The Bedford lorry would nowadays be a write off but in wartime it might well have undergone extensive repairs, for vehicles of any sort were in short supply. Photograph courtesy Peter Newland.

On 26 April 1948 tram No.64 on Route 2 (East Park Road via London Road) is pursued by No.165 on Route 3 Stoneygate. The 1936 Morris 8 takes refuge at the entrance to Charles Street. The 'hut' on the corner car park was an outlet for 'Eric's Ice Cream'. The YMCA behind in East Street is still used by that association. The former 'Harris of Granby Corner' furniture shop and the City Police Station in Charles Street (opened in 1933) still exist but the road priorities have completely changed. Granby Street is now one way and all traffic takes a right turn onto a newly constructed fly-over – Waterloo Way and St Georges Way. Photograph Leicester Mercury.

CLARENDON PARK ROUTE.
(*Via London Road*).

Clarendon Park Tramcars from either terminus every 4, 4½, 5 and 6 minutes (via London Road).

		Weekdays.	Saturdays.	Sundays.
First Car—Clock Tower	..	6. 8 a.m.	6. 8 a.m.	9.41 a.m.
,, ,, Welford Road	..	6.25 a.m.	6.25 a.m.	10. 0 a.m.
Last Car—Clock Tower	..	11. 0 p.m.	11.19 p.m.	10.45 p.m.
,, ,, Welford Road	..	11.18 p.m.	11.37 p.m.	11. 3 p.m.

Below. On 16 December 1948 Nos.72 and 6, both rebuilt in the early 1930s with extended frames, await passengers at the Clarendon Park Terminus in Welford Road. No.6 displays the correct destination – Blackbird Road – while No.72 still shows the Clarendon Park destination. It was one of twelve rebuilds fitted with transverse leather seats on the lower deck. The *art deco* building is the Knighton Kinema opened in 1937; it closed in 1963 and the site has been redeveloped. Photograph A.D. Packer.

In the post-war years David Packer recorded the Leicester Tramway scene, particularly on 16 December 1948. By this date the system was in steep decline. With total closure but eleven months away a deterioration in the appearance of the trams was only too apparent. This is Clarendon Park terminus again, closed on 13 March 1949; on 16 December the previous year the crews of No.78 (with extended frames and upholstered seats on the same day as above) and No.70 await passengers and a return to the Clock Tower and then onwards to Blackbird Road. No.70 bears evidence of wartime window repairs on the lower deck rear platform. The air raid shelter is just visible outside the Knighton Kinema. Photograph A.D. Packer.

Braunstone Gate/West Bridge was little photographed in tramway days but in 1946 No.118 can be seen returning from Narborough Road, heading to the Clock Tower and then Route 2 Melton Road. The large factory beyond belonged to Frisby-Jarvis hosiery manufacturers. Case's Cash Stores is on the left. The adverts on the right tell us that 'Duel in the Sun' was the feature film showing at the Savoy Cinema in Belgrave Gate, one of the city's best picture houses.

On 30 October 1949, ten days before closure of the Leicester Tramways, No.129 returns from Humberstone to the Clock Tower on Uppingham Road. The shop on the corner of St Barnabas Road is Worthingtons, a chain of grocers which could once be found in every district of the city. Their sales slogan was 'Let Worthingtons feed you' during the years of food rationing and that is what they did – provided you were a registered customer. The heavy overhead is surplus cable from the East Park Road route which until closure on 15 May 1949 turned into St Barnabas Road at this point. The lack of petrol (on ration at a gallon per week for a small family car) ensured a virtual absence of motor cars from the roads. Photograph R.B. Parr.

TRAMCAR SERVICES.

HUMBERSTONE AND COLEMAN ROAD ROUTES.

Humberstone Tramcars from either terminus every 4 and 5½ minutes.

	Weekdays.	Saturdays.	Sundays.
First Car—Clock Tower ..	6. 5 a.m.	6. 5 a.m.	9.39 a.m.
,, ,, Terminus ..	6.21 a.m.	6.21 a.m.	9.55 a.m.
Last Car—Clock Tower ..	11. 3 p.m.	11.19½ p.m.	10.45½ p.m.
,, ,, Terminus ..	11.19 p.m.	11.35½ p.m.	11.1½ p.m.

Coleman Road Tramcars from either terminus every 11 and 16 minutes.

First Car—Clock Tower ..	6.22 a.m.	6.22 a.m.	9.42 a.m.
,, ,, Terminus ..	6.39 a.m.	6.39 a.m.	9.58 a.m.
Last Car—Clock Tower ..	11. 0 p.m.	11.17 p.m.	10.46 p.m.
,, ,, Terminus ..	11.17 p.m.	11.34 p.m.	11. 2 p.m.

The trams were every effective for moving masses of passengers, especially as they ran at intervals of three minutes or so. In September 1941 crowds are queuing opposite the Victoria Park Gates on London Road after a meeting of Jehovah's Witnesses at De Montfort Hall. The unidentified leading car is on Route 3 Stoneygate and No.135 is on a Route 4 working to Clarendon Park. The word 'Leicester' was erased from every tram (and bus) just in case a German invasion came, in the hope that the enemy might be unaware of their location! Photograph courtesy Peter Newland.

No electricity – maybe a power cut or a fuse failure meant no trams. This 1947 view shows seven cars at a standstill due to some such problem; this was a serious matter indeed, for Leicester was still heavily dependent on its trams – they provided some two thirds of the public transport services at this time. The trams are well cared for, especially No.137 and the following car No.25; the deterioration in external cleanliness did not come until the final year of operation, 1948-49. Photograph Leicester Mercury.

Above. The Shipstone Arms in Hinckley Road in 1947 with No.138, a tram with extended frames and transverse lower deck seating, on a Light Railway Transport League tour of the system, which was then still largely intact. There is no evidence that the tram was on a pub crawl! Honestly, it had merely stopped to pick up some enthusiasts who may have been inspecting the trackwork and ancillary installations at this junction with the Narborough Road line. No.138 was a well-photographed tram, often used for special tours of the system. It was withdrawn on the final day of operation – 9 November 1949.

Left. What appears to be a posed photograph outside Lewis's store in Humberstone Gate on 13 July 1938, with the conductor about to unhook the trolley pole while the driver looks at the photographer. No.141 is in immaculate condition – typical of the pre-war appearance of all Leicester's trams, in either livery. All the Humberstone Gate buildings have since been demolished; the Haymarket Centre occupies the right-hand side while Lewis's store (built in 1936) has also succumbed .

A bizarre accident occurred just south of the Midland Station on 27 October 1948, when No.47 was lifted off the southbound track in a collision with a towed ex-Army vehicle and thrown at right angles across the road. Traffic was diverted into Conduit Street by Richardson's surgical shop and it took the combined efforts of the City Transport Crossley breakdown truck and Tram No.87 (hurrying to the scene) to re-rail it. Damage was superficial but as always an accident attracted the crowds. Photograph Leicester Mercury.

A 1937 view of Humberstone Gate taken shortly after the completion of Lewis's Department Store, with No.149 on Route 7 from Humberstone approaching its terminus outside the great store, at 11.45am on a bright sunny day. Only the *art deco* tower now survives as a memorial to a splendid departmental store. Maxwells on the left sold ladies fashions, while W.A. Lea & Son on the right-hand corner was a high class clothing, hosiery and haberdashery store. All that remains of this scene apart from Lewis's Tower are one or two buildings including the former Burton's the Tailor premises, at the far end of the photograph, on the left.

An ex-War Department Bedford truck has collided with car 155 outside the LMS station, inevitably bringing traffic to a virtual standstill. The driver's mate in the Lindley & Lindley 1932 Leyland lorry guides his driver past the incident, while a group of onlookers watch the proceedings with interest. The road haulage vehicles still bear the remnants of the white markings on mudguards or front wings – a wartime measure dating the photo to the 1946/47 winter. Photograph Leicester Mercury.

A busy 1948 scene in Evington Road/St Stephens Road. With Barclays Bank on the left tram No.157 squeezes between a 1939 Morris 12 CJF 619 and a 1939 Rover 10 (FXN 482 London registered). This was the East Park Road Route which had a number of passing loops; No.157 is leaving one of these for Victoria Park Gates, where it will head down London Road and on to the Clock Tower.

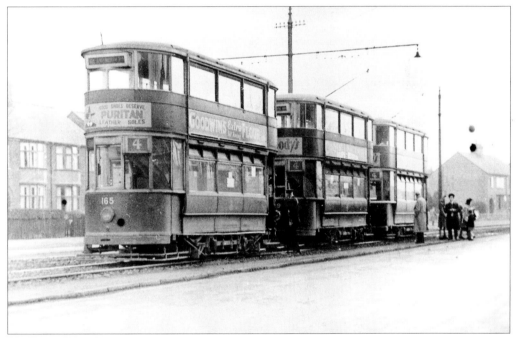

Blackbird Road late in 1948, with three stationary trams. No.165 may be the cause of the hold up as its trolley pole has been lowered from the overhead wire which provides the current. Some crew members between the disabled car and No.129 (the middle tram) appear to be in earnest discussion. All the trams display Route 4 (Clarendon Park) and will have to wait until 165 is towed away.

No.168 on war service on 25 February 1942, disguised as HMS Renown for a £200,000 appeal to the good citizens of Leicester. It is standing outside the Abbey Park Road Tram Depot. The name chosen was appropriate as the Corporation ran a fleet of AEC 'Renown' six wheeled buses, the last of the type to be built. (No.329 of this type of bus has been superbly restored by Leicestershire Museums).

Above. No.167 in a quiet moment in 1949 at Humberstone Drive, before reversing for the return journey to the Clock Tower. A group of parents and children walk towards Scraptoft Lane and maybe the 'Trocadero Cinema'. Photograph R. Carter.

Left. Easter Saturday 1938; tram No.177 loads to capacity on a service to Stoneygate Route 3 while No.56 follows behind on Route 1 (East Park Road via London Road). The wedding car (an Armstrong Siddeley of about 1930) is followed by ARY 246, a 1936 Standard 9. Heading towards the Clock Tower in a queue is an Austin 12 tourer dating from 1931, preceded by a 1936 Morris 8 (CON 870) – motor car design changed radically during the 1930s. The newspaper placard refers to a disastrous Good Friday match when Wolverhampton Wanderers defeated Leicester City 10-1! Photograph Leicester Mercury.

TRAMCAR SERVICES.

THE STONEYGATE ROUTE.

Stoneygate Tramcars from either Terminus every 4, 4½, 5 and 6 minutes.

	Weekdays.	Saturdays.	Sundays.
First Car—Clock Tower ..	6.12 a.m.	6.12 a.m.	9.38 a.m.
,, ,, Terminus ..	6.30 a.m.	6.30 a.m.	9.57 a.m.
Last Car—Clock Tower ..	11.2½ p.m.	11.16½ p.m.	10.47 p.m.
,, ,, Terminus ..	11.23½ p.m.	11.37½ p.m.	11. 8 p.m.

Below. A wintry view of tram No.6 on 16 December 1948. It was working Route 4 to Blackbird Road and is pictured in Eastgates, having just passed the Clock Tower. Berrys fish, game and poultry shop is on the left and the Eclipse public house, owned by Shipstones Brewery, is almost hidden (eclipsed even!) by the tram. Corts Ltd occupied the corner of Silver Street and Market Place for several decades. The policeman on point duty seems to have no pedestrians or road vehicles to control. As in so many towns and cities 'pedestrianisation' has now taken place in the centre of Leicester, with access for public service vehicles only. Photo A.D. Packer.

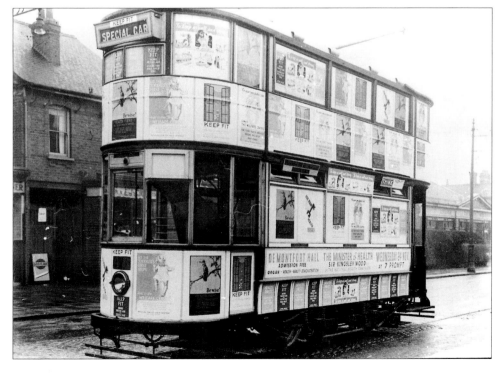

Leicester had a tradition of decorating tramcars for special events and this view of No.48 at the Aylestone terminus in November 1938 shows it covered with posters extolling the virtues of keeping fit. It draws attention as well, to a free health and beauty demonstration due to take place at the De Montfort Hall, with (and this seems hardly credible) the Minister of Health in attendance. Photograph Leicestershire Museums.

TRAMCAR SERVICES.

THE BLACKBIRD ROAD AND GROBY ROAD,
is an outer route that skirts the north-west side of the City between Belgrave Road and Fosse Road (North).

Blackbird and Groby Roads Tramcars from either terminus every 10, 15 and 30 minutes at certain periods of the day.

		Weekdays.	Saturdays.	Sundays.
First Car—Abbey Park Road		6.55 a.m.	6.55 a.m.	10.30 a.m.
,, ,, Groby Road	..	7.10 a.m.	7.10 a.m.	10.45½ a.m.
Last Car—Abbey Park Road		11. 0 p.m.	11. 0 p.m.	10. 0 p.m.
,, ,, Groby Road	..	11.15 p.m.	11.15 p.m.	10.15 p.m.

On Sundays, a Service also operates between **Groby Road Terminus** and **Clock Tower**, *via* Sanvey Gate as follows :—

First Car—Clock Tower	..	1.20 p.m.
,, ,, Groby Road	..	1.45 p.m.
Last Car—Clock Tower	..	5.20 p.m.
,, ,, Groby Road	..	5.42 p.m.

Below. Evington Road on a bright winter's day in 1948. Tram No.84 has entered one of several passing loops on the largely single track section of the East Park Route at the junction of Abingdon Road. A sturdy 1932 Morris Isis JU 221 follows the tram towards the London Road Victoria Park Gates Junction. Photograph F.N.T. L.L. Jones.

About 1948 tram No.93 has just entered the reserved track which ran along Blackbird Road. Woodgates, Groby Road and Fosse Road all converged to the left of the right-hand block of shops. The tram does at least display its ultimate destination, Route No.4 Clarendon Park, which it will reach by going in a clockwise direction into Abbey Park Road, Belgrave Road, Clock Tower and London Road to its terminus in Welford Road. Photograph F.N.T. L.L. Jones.

TRAMCAR SERVICES.

EAST PARK ROAD ROUTE.

East Park Road Tramcars from Clock Tower either way every 3, 3½, 4, 4½, 5 and 6 minutes. (Circular Route).

	Weekdays.	Saturdays.	Sundays.
First Car—East Park *via* London Road	6.15 a.m.	6.15 a.m.	9.41 a.m.
,, ,, East Park *via* Humberstone Rd.	6.10 a.m.	6.10 a.m.	9.38½ a.m.
Last Car—East Park *via* London Road ..	11. 3 p.m.	11.17 p.m.	10.47 p.m.
,, ,, East Park *via* Humberstone Rd.	11.0½ p.m.	11.15 p.m.	10.45 p.m.

Below. Tram 97 in Uppingham Road about 1948, on an East Park Road circular route. The villas are better than the usual terrace housing in Leicester and would have been much sought after by the middle-classes at the turn of the century. Photograph F.N.T. L.L. Jones.

Tram No.110 was the last car running in pre-1937 livery, which it retained until withdrawal in October 1949. It is seen here in late 1948 on a Route 9 Groby Road service at the Abbey Lane Junction. Period road signs are much in evidence though only one car is in sight, a Morris 8 series E, the predecessor to the post-war Morris Minor. The scene at this time was relatively undeveloped and quiet. Photograph F.N.T. L.L. Jones.

Winter 1948, and tram No.117 is at the junction with Haynes Road, outward bound to Humberstone Terminus. At this relatively late stage in the tramway's life, the setts (more often known as 'cobbles' these days) are somewhat uneven and tarmac has been used to make repairs. The one pedestrian appears to be a door to door salesman; his wares are not easily identifiable though brushes would be a fair bet! Photograph F.N.T. L.L. Jones.

By October 1949 Humberstone was the sole surviving route. Tram No.117 is crossing the Charles Street Junction chasing a battered 1937 Hillman Minx. The shape of things to come are the two AEC Regent III buses parked outside the Palais de Danse, the nearest one being No.7, FBC 274 delivered in July 1949.

Tram No.135 emerges from Abbey Park Road on route 4 – Clarendon Park via London Road – in the winter of 1948. The appearance of the trams at this late stage was in sharp contrast to the sparkling condition of pre-war days. An Austin 7 tourer of about 1936 is turning into Belgrave Road past Cundys decorating shop. This road still exists, but as a cul-de-sac – a new junction having been constructed to cater for modern road traffic conditions. Photograph F.N.T. L.L. Jones.

Blackbird Road in the winter of 1948 and, judging from the prominent clothesline, a Monday washday. Tram No.158 is travelling clockwise on the reserved track displaying Route 4 (Clarendon Park), its ultimate destination on the south side of the city. A large plot of land is up for sale on the left, either for industrial or private development. Road vehicles are absent as petrol was virtually unobtainable. The country had to 'export or die' to earn US dollars, essential currency for the purchase of oil. Leicester was fortunate indeed to still have some of its tramway system operating at this difficult time. Photograph F.N.T. L.L. Jones.

This view of Welford Place around 1920 shows tram No.5 emerging from Belvoir Street, about to pass the statue of John Biggs, a local dignitary. The building on the left was the head office of the Leicester Permanent Building Society. Walter Osborne's Billiard Saloon is prominently advertised in the right foreground and on a sunny and warm day a workman is pushing his handcart over the tramlines and cobbles. The imposing building to the right of the tram belonged to the Phoenix Insurance Co. Ltd.; John Biggs himself was thrice Mayor of Leicester in the nineteenth century. Photograph A.P. Newland Collection.

WESTERN PARK ROUTE.

Western Park Tramcars from either terminus every 3, 3½, 4, 4½, 5 and 6 minutes.

	Weekdays.	Saturdays.	Sundays.
First Car—Clock Tower	6.15 a.m.	6.15 a.m.	9.40 a.m.
„ „ Terminus	6.29 a.m.	6.29 a.m.	9.54 a.m.
Last Car—Clock Tower	11. 2 p.m.	11.15 p.m.	10.48 p.m.
„ „ Terminus	11.16 p.m.	11.29 p.m.	11. 2 p.m.

Top right. Humberstone Gate in 1937, and tram No.132 is passing a rather neglected and dirty Morris 8 hp 4 door saloon. The rear numberplate is held by one nut and bolt only; ARY 237, registered in Leicester in June 1936, was probably purchased from H.A. Hamshaw Ltd – the main Morris distributor. Their premises were in Humberstone Gate on the right and behind the new Morris 18 hp which is following tram No.28 (of 1904 vintage). No.28, in its turn, is heading for the High Street loading barrier and then to Western Park, Route No.1. Photograph National Tramway Museum, H.B. Priestley Collection.

Left. Horsefair Street was rarely photographed as service trams ceased to use the tracks after 1934. The *raison d'être* was to enable Aylestone and Clarendon Park (via Welford Road) trams to return to the Abbey Park Road Depot at the end of the day. In this view taken at 12.35pm on 3 May 1939 road traffic dominates and two City Transport buses are passing each other – with difficulty. No.306, a 1937 Leyland TD4C gearless vehicle is on a No.26 Knighton Lane service while No.267 (JF 5009) is on a Melbourne Road service. It was one of the earliest diesel engined Leyland buses, delivered new in December 1933. Photograph A.P. Newland Collection.

Above. Tram No.54 resplendent in the new livery, in Welford Place, passing the statue of John Biggs (three times Mayor of Leicester) on the left and about to turn into Welford Road en route to Aylestone. The car parked outside Franks Furniture and Pram Shop is a 1933 Hillman Minx, the van a 1930 Morris 10cwt with artillery wheels. The tall gable in the left distance proudly marks the premises of Joseph Johnson, a well known fashion and departmental store, now Fenwicks. Photograph National Tramway Museum, H.B. Priestley Collection.

CLARENDON PARK ROUTE.
(*Via Welford Road*).

Clarendon Park Tramcars from either terminus every 5, 6 and 9 minutes at certain periods of the day. (Via Welford Road).

	Weekdays.	*Saturdays.*	*Sundays.*
First Car—Bowling Green St.	7. 3 a.m.	7. 3 a.m.	2.25 p.m.
,, ,, Welford Road ..	7.17 a.m.	7.17 a.m.	2.37 p.m.
Last Car—Bowling Green St.	6.26 p.m.	1.22 p.m.	5. 5 p.m.
,, ,, Welford Road ..	6.41 p.m.	1.37 p.m.	5.17 p.m.

Leicester's sole surviving railway station, in London Road, was built by the Midland Railway to the design of Charles Trubshaw in 1892. It replaced the original station in Campbell Street. In this 1938 view tram No.169 (built in 1920 by the United Electric Car Co, Preston) is loading passengers for Stoneygate at the barrier outside the station. A 1937 SS Jaguar is attempting to gain entrance to the car park inside the station, by this time owned by the LMS. Now a listed building, the magnificent facade has been fully restored and no longer displays the advertising hoardings which used to detract so much from its appearance. Photograph National Tramway Museum, H.B. Priestley.

The Clarendon Park route terminated in Welford Road where No.66 is pictured on 16 December 1948. The gas street lamps beyond the terminus are already lit on this gloomy day. The shops (under different ownership) still exist and the general scene is largely unchanged. Photograph A.D. Packer.

In the winter of 1948-49 No.2 enters a passing loop in Clarendon Park Road, near to Avenue Road. Chamberlain's cycle shop is on the left and the tram will merely pause in the loop and wait for another to pass in the opposite direction. The scene is little altered and, remarkably, a cycle shop still exists on the spot; only the trams are no more. The route closed on 15 March 1949. Photograph F.N.T. L.L. Jones.

TRAMCAR SERVICES.

BELGRAVE & MELTON ROAD ROUTES.

Belgrave Tramcars from either terminus every 3, 3½, 4, 4½, 5 and 6 minutes.

	Weekdays.	Saturdays.	Sundays.
First Car—Clock Tower ..	6.10 a.m.	6.10 a.m.	9.38 a.m.
,, ,, Terminus ..	6.26½ a.m.	6.26½ a.m.	9.37 a.m.
Last Car—Clock Tower ..	11. 0 p.m.	11.16 p.m.	10.48 p.m.
,, ,, Terminus ..	11.14 p.m.	11.30 p.m.	11. 1 p.m.

Melton Road Tramcars from either Terminus every 3, 3½, 4, 4½, 5 and 6 minutes.

	Weekdays.	Saturdays.	Sundays.
First Car—Clock Tower ..	6.15 a.m.	6.15 a.m.	9.40½ a.m.
,, ,, Terminus ..	6.29 a.m.	6.29 a.m.	9.40½ a.m.
Last Car—Clock Tower ..	11.2½ p.m.	11.18 p.m.	10.46 p.m.
,, ,, Terminus ..	11.17½ p.m.	11.33 p.m.	11. 0 p.m.

Below. On a sunny day in 1938 tram No.42 awaits at the Aylestone route central terminus in Bowling Green Street. To the left stands the rear part of the Town Hall while three motor cars, a Model C Ford 10, a Vauxhall 10 and a Jowett take advantage of the parking afforded by the track merging with the single running line.

Belgrave Terminus on 23 June 1937, and tram No.63 is in typically immaculate condition as it awaits departure for the Clock Tower and then East Park Road (Route 1 via London Road). A barrow and ladder on the left belong to the local window cleaner. Brayshaw & Carrs garage on the right displays a 'Tecalamit' lubrication sign. This service using Mobil oils and grease was popular when cars needed greasing at 500 mile intervals and an engine oil change was recommended at every 1000 miles! Two Morris cars are on the forecourt; a February 1937 Morris 8 four door saloon, registered in Middlesex and a 1933 Morris Minor tourer – OJ 6587 which started life in Birmingham. Photograph National Tramway Museum, H.B. Priestley.

Knighton Kinema had only just been opened when this picture was taken on 25 May 1938. Tram No.94 on Route 5 (Clarendon Park via Welford Road) is fitted with additional braking (known as slipper brakes) for use on the descent down Cemetery Hill – a steeply graded and curving line which passed over the LMS railway line to St Pancras, London. The 'Kinema' was demolished in 1963 to make way for a modern supermarket. Over sixty years later, the terraced housing and shops, built in large numbers at the turn of the nineteenth century, still exist. The area indeed has changed little since this picture was taken by Henry Priestley. Photograph National Tramway Museum, H.B. Priestley.

At the St Barnabas Road Junction Tram No.153 (and in the post-1937 livery, on Route No.7) pauses on Uppingham Road to pick up a passenger on 25 May 1938. The railway bridge carries the ex-GNR line from Belgrave Road station which meandered through the Leicestershire Wolds to Melton Mowbray and on to Lincolnshire and the east coast resorts of Skegness and Mablethorpe. Photograph National Tramway Museum, H.B. Priestley.

In September 1941 one of the 1924 Leyland tower lorries with solid tyres is parked in the centre of London Road at the Victoria Park Gates, affording some attention to the overhead lines. The lighting equipment on the lorry has been altered in strict accordance with wartime regulations. The side lights have been masked and the nearside headlamp has an obscure wartime fitment ensuring that the light (if any) was directed to the road. The offside head lamp glass has been painted over and bears the letters ARP (Air Raid Precautions) and this vehicle was undoubtedly used for repairs to the overhead at night-time. Those queuing for city-bound trams have attended a Jehovah's Witness meeting at the nearby De Montfort Hall. Road traffic is inevitably sparse. The large Hillman limousine turning into Granville Road was registered in Halifax in 1936 and was still in use despite strict petrol rationing (it only did about 12mpg). Photograph Peter Newland Collection.

Above. A newly overhauled tram, No.136 resplendent in its new livery of maroon with cream window frames and as yet unfettered by advertisements, at Melton Turn (at the junction of Melton Road and Loughborough Road) on 25 May 1938. It is about to pick up passengers outside Mr W.A. Israel's tobacco shop. The road to the right of the tram is Doncaster Road. Behind is the sort of 'corner shop' bank branch now becoming an endangered species. Photograph National Tramway Museum, H.B. Priestley.

Left. An aerial view of London Road taken in the summer of 1947, possibly from the roof of Leah Marks whose ladies' gown shop was on the corner of Waterloo Street. An unidentified tram is preceded by a Bedford OB van, while heading up London Road an Alfred Davies van is turning into Nelson Street, halting the progress of two trams, No.101 behind and No.7 coming downhill. No.7 is followed by a lorry, van, car and a Leyland bus. On this sunny day a horsedrawn cart avoids the parked cars and tram tracks. The buildings still exist largely unaltered, although the pavements are narrower on what is the A6 London Road. Photograph D.R. Harvey Collection.

An unidentified tram parked outside the White Hart Hotel in Haymarket, the central pickup point for the East Park Road route via London Road. From the passengers' headgear the photograph probably dates from the 1920s; the appearance of the tram is identical to the preserved No.76 at the National Tramway Museum at Crich. Photograph A.D. Packer.

A busy scene in 1938 in High Street. Three Morris cars, a 1936 Morris 8HP, 1935 10HP and a 1938 12/4HP compete for road space with the immaculately maintained trams, both in their original livery. No.106 is on Route 9 (Groby Road) which it will reach by the long way, via Abbey Park Road. No.152 (to the right) is on a short Route 3 working to Great Central Street and the LNER station. Clemersons Ltd on the left corner was a high class furnisher, while Pratts shop behind BJF 527 had two businesses, an aquatics division and a seed shop. Photograph National Tramway Museum, H.B. Priestley.

On 25 June 1937 tram No.7, one of twenty-three rebuilt with extended frames in the early 1930s and resplendent in the original livery, has stopped at the top of King Richard's Road for passengers to disembark, prior to turning into Fosse Road (Central). In a then primarily residential area, only one villa has been converted to commercial use, by E. Bax & Co, builders and contractors. The pedestrians are smartly dressed and on the upper deck male passengers are seen with typical caps on their heads. The old saying, 'if you want to get ahead, get a hat', actually meant something, and was certainly employed by Dunn & Co, a chain of high class Gents outfitters, which only recently has become extinct. Photograph National Tramway Museum, M.J. O'Connor.

A busy scene at Evington Road at the junction with London Road, opposite Victoria Park Gates, 25 May 1938. Tram No.27 is on Route 1 (East Park Road via London Road) and No.37, about to emerge onto London Road towards the station, is on a Route 2 Narborough Road working. An Austin 'Big Seven' CDF 734 is turning into Evington Road while DJH99, an Austin 12, appears to be overtaking No.37 on the inside. Both are 1937 cars; in the background a 1935 Morris 8 NV 6128 registered in Northampton awaits its turn. The buildings still exist and the junction is now awash with traffic lights. In the early 1950s after the closure of the tramways, roundabouts were thought to be the solution to traffic congestion – at the time floral displays were provided by the Parks Department. Photograph National Tramway Museum, H.B. Priestley.

Left. Tram No.47 was one of the first to be painted in the newly revised livery introduced in 1937. The fleet number was originally applied as shown, together with the legend under the side number 'LEICESTER CITY TRANSPORT B.ENGLAND GENERAL MANAGER AND ENGINEER' – just about visible in this picture. Later on the legend was transferred to the other end of the courtesy panel and the tram number lowered to the original legend position. Seen in the autumn of 1938 at Narborough Road terminus No.47 displays the additional destination boards on the lower deck. In reality these were an operational hindrance and often confused the travelling public. The motor car behind is one of the earliest Morris 8 Series E Models, introduced in September 1938. It was a popular vehicle, produced after the war until 1948, when the immortal 'Morris Minor' designed by Alec Issigonis, superseded it. Photograph National Tramway Museum, M.J. O'Connor.

Below. 'Works Carts' (known variously as 'water wagons', 'knife grinders' and so on) were rarely seen in action during daylight hours, their principal activities taking place after nightfall when they cleansed the tracks of the inevitable debris which collected during the day, litter, road grit and so on. Leicester had three such vehicles, each carrying a large water tank, the contents of which were applied under pressure to clean the grooves of the running lines. No.181 had a collapsible tower fitted and was used principally on the Blackbird Road central reservation for all kinds of maintenance. Parked behind is No.180, a conventional water cart. Spare BRILL 21E trucks are parked in various stages of repair – picture taken in the Abbey Park Road Depot about 1937. Photograph W.A. Jackman Collection.

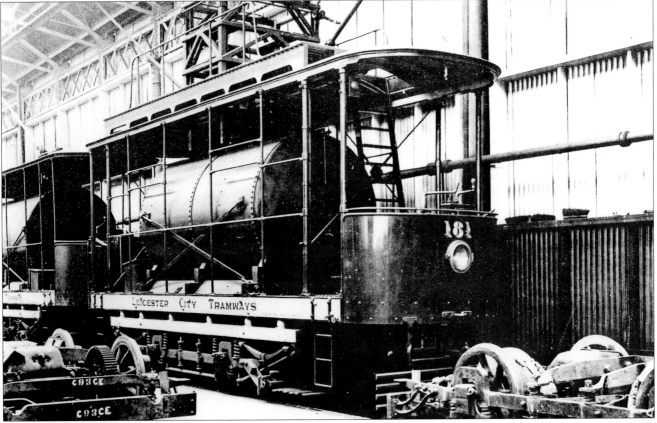